Sports Illustrated KID$

THE ULTIMATE GUIDE TO PRO FOOTBALL TEAMS

by Shane Frederick

CAPSTONE PRESS
a capstone imprint

Sports Illustrated KIDS Ultimate Pro Team Guides are published
by Capstone Press, 151 Good Counsel Drive, P.O. Box 669,
Mankato, Minnesota 56002. www.capstonepub.com

102010
005987R

Books published by Capstone Press are manufactured with
paper containing at least 10 percent post-consumer waste.

Library of Congress Cataloging-in-Publication Data
Frederick, Shane.
 The ultimate guide to pro football teams / by Shane Frederick.
   p. cm.—(Sports Illustrated KIDS. Ultimate pro guides)
 Includes index.
 ISBN 978-1-4296-4819-6 (library binding)
 ISBN 978-1-4296-5642-9 (paperback)
 1. Football—Juvenile literature. 2. Football teams—Juvenile
literature. 3. National Football League—Juvenile literature.
 I. Title. II. Series.
 GV950.7.F74 2010
  796.332'64—dc22   2010009998

Editorial Credits: Anthony Wacholtz, editor; Tracy Davies, designer;
Eric Gohl, media researcher; Laura Manthe, production specialist

Image Credits: Getty Images Inc.: Doug Pensinger, 5 (t); iStockphoto:
Photoroller (field), 2, 68–69; Newscom: 11 (b), 19 (t), 25 (t), 46 (b), 64
(b), Icon SMI/Chuck Solomon, 7 (t), KRT/Kansas City Star/Fernando
Salazar, 35 (b); Shutterstock: Adam Derewecki, 19 (b), Danny E Hooks
(chalkboard diagram), cover, doodle (shattered glass), back cover, 68,
kots, cover (bl), Pell Studio (football), cover, back cover, 1, 68, Photoroller
(field), cover, back cover, 70, 72, Tomasz Sowinski, design element; Sports
Illustrated: Al Tielemans, 9 (t), 12 (b), 18 (t), 26 (b), 29 (t), 30 (t), 32 (all),
34 (t), 40 (b), 46 (t), 50 (t), 52 (t), 62 (t), 63 (t), 64 (t), Andy Hayt, 48 (b),
57 (t), 60 (b), 66 (b), Bill Frakes, 1, 13 (b), 33 (all), 37 (t), 41 (b), 61 (b),
Bob Rosato, cover (br), 5 (b), 12 (t), 13 (b), 14 (t), 27 (t), 28 (b), 29 (b),
31 (t), 37 (b), 40 (t), 43 (b), 51 (t), 60 (t), 62 (b), 63 (b), 65 (b), Damian
Strohmeyer, cover (bm), 7 (b), 10 (all), 20 (b), 23 (b), 24 (t), 26 (t), 31 (b),
34 (b), 39 (b), 45 (all), 51 (b), 52 (b), 65 (t), Heinz Kluetmeier, 6 (b), 8 (b),
9 (b), 15 (b), 27 (b), 53 (t), 56 (b), 67 (t), Hy Peskin, 18 (b), 24 (b), John
Biever, 6 (t), 14 (b), 16 (t), 17 (t), 30 (b), 38 (t), John Iacono, 11 (t), 15 (t),
17 (b), 22 (t), 35 (t), 39 (t), 41 (t), 44 (b), 47 (b), John G. Zimmerman,
50 (b), John W. McDonough, 4 (t), 28 (t), 54 (all), 55 (t), 59 (b), Lane
Stewart, 21 (b), Manny Millan, 42 (b), Mark Kauffman, 25 (b), Peter
Read Miller, 2, 21 (t), 22 (b), 56 (t), 58 (all), 61 (t), Robert Beck, 23 (t), 44
(t), 47 (t), 49 (b), 55 (t), 59 (t), Simon Bruty, 8 (t), 20 (t), 36 (t), 42 (t), 43
(t), 66 (t), V.J. Lovero, 4 (b), 48 (t), Walter Iooss Jr., 16 (b), 36 (b), 38 (b),
49 (t), 53 (b), 57 (b); Wikipedia: Bernard Gagnon, 67 (b).

TABLE OF CONTENTS

THE SUPER BOWL is the ultimate football game. It's the final game of an exciting, hard-hitting season that keeps fans coming back each week and each season.

In 2010 more people watched the big game than any other television program in history. In that game, quarterback Drew Brees and the New Orleans Saints upset Peyton Manning and the Indianapolis Colts 31-17. The Saints overcame a history of losing and inspired their fans, many of whom were still recovering from the devastation of Hurricane Katrina four and a half years earlier.

Football is the most popular sport in America. Teams are found in big cities such as New York City and smaller towns such as Green Bay, Wisconsin. The fans cheer in the New England snow and the Florida heat. They watch an old team in Chicago and a newer team in Houston. It's been that way for decades, even before the days of instant replay, domed stadiums, and fantasy football.

Fans watch each week hoping to see bruising runs, bullet passes, and bone-rattling hits. They cheer for tiptoe catches, pick-six interceptions, and quarterback sacks. By the end of the 16-game season and intense playoffs, fans hope their team is one of the final two that get to the Super Bowl. And, of course, they hope their team is the one hoisting the silver, football-shaped trophy at the end.

ARIZONA CARDINALS

Franchise Record: 483–680–39

Home Field:
University of Phoenix Stadium
(63,400 capacity) in Glendale, Arizona

CHAMPIONSHIPS
1925, 1947

First Season: 1898

The Cardinals franchise is the oldest in the NFL. But it wasn't always in the desert. The team started out of an athletic club in Chicago, Illinois. They got their nickname—the Cardinals—in 1901 because of their red jerseys. They were known as the Chicago Cardinals when they joined the NFL in the 1920s. The Cardinals began their move west in 1960, first stopping in St. Louis, Missouri. Then they moved to Arizona in 1988.

Legends & Stars

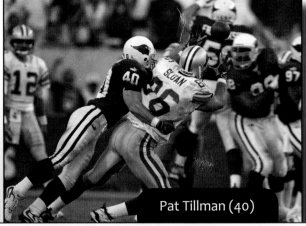

Pat Tillman (40)

Dan Dierdorf	OL	1971–1983	Played in six Pro Bowl games in seven seasons
Larry Fitzgerald	WR	2004–present	Three-time Pro Bowl wide receiver
Ernie Nevers	HB	1929–1931	Nevers was inducted into the Hall of Fame in 1963; the halfback could kick field goals and extra points too
Jackie Smith	TE	1963–1977	Started at tight end for 15 straight years
Pat Tillman	S	1998–2001	Became a national hero by giving up a promising football career to join the U.S. Army in 2002; he died after being deployed in Afghanistan
Charley Trippi	RB	1947–1955	Scored two touchdowns in the 1947 title game

By the Numbers

TOP PASSER	**Jim Hart** 1966–1983 34,639 yards	**TOP RUSHER** **Ottis Anderson** 1979–1986 7,999 yards
TOP RECEIVER	**Roy Green** 1979–1990 8,496 yards	**MOST TDS SCORED** **Roy Green** 69 TDs

Point Man

In 1929 the Cardinals' player-coach Ernie Nevers made history by scoring every point for his team in a 40-6 win over the Bears. Nevers scored six touchdowns and kicked four extra points. A week later he scored every point in a 19-0 victory to score 59 consecutive points for the Cardinals.

Larry Fitzgerald celebrates a touchdown catch during Super Bowl XLIII.

Waiting for a Winner

Despite being around for more than 100 years, the Cardinals have won only two championships, both as the Chicago Cardinals. They also played in the Super Bowl following the 2008 season.

ATLANTA FALCONS

First Season: 1966

Franchise Record: 276–390–6

Home Field: Georgia Dome
(71,228 capacity) in Atlanta, Georgia

CHAMPIONSHIPS
None

Since first taking flight in the mid-1960s, the Atlanta Falcons have had their share of exciting players. From Steve Bartkowski in the 1970s and '80s to Matt Ryan in the late 2000s, Falcons quarterbacks have always made opposing defenses a little nervous.

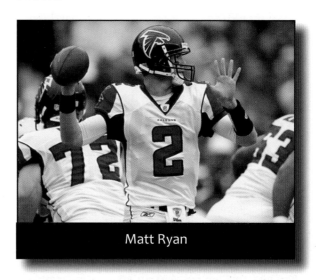

Matt Ryan

Legends & Stars

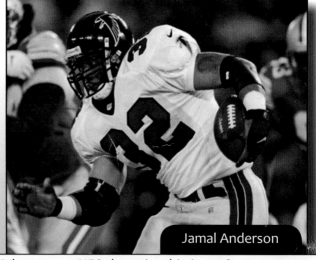

Jamal Anderson

Jamal Anderson	RB	1994–2001	Led Atlanta to an NFC championship in 1998
Steve Bartkowski	QB	1975–1985	1975 Rookie of the Year is the team's career passing leader
Matt Ryan	QB	2008–present	Rookie of the Year in 2008
Deion Sanders	CB	1989–1993	Scored touchdowns on offense, defense, and special teams
Jessie Tuggle	LB	1987–2000	Five-time Pro Bowl selection is Falcons' career leader in tackles

By the Numbers

TOP PASSER	**Steve Bartkowski** 1975–1985 23,470 yards	**TOP RUSHER**	**Gerald Riggs** 1982–1988 6,631 yards
TOP RECEIVER	**Terance Mathis** 1994–2001 7,349 yards	**MOST TDS SCORED**	**Terance Mathis** 57 TDs

Unlikely Underdog

In 1998 the Falcons finished the regular season 14–2. They faced the powerful Minnesota Vikings, who were 15–1 in the regular season, in the NFC championship game. Atlanta trailed 27-17 in the fourth quarter but rallied to tie the game and force overtime. The reliable Morten Andersen kicked a 38-yard field goal and put the Falcons into the Super Bowl for the first time in franchise history.

Tony Martin makes an over-the-head catch in the 1998 NFC championship game.

Prime Time Player

Falcons cornerback "Prime Time" Deion Sanders was a two-sport athlete. In 1989 he became the only player to hit a major league baseball home run and score an NFL touchdown in the same week.

BALTIMORE RAVENS

Franchise Record: 116–107–1

HOME FIELD: M&T Bank Stadium
(70,107 capacity) in Baltimore, Maryland

CHAMPIONSHIP
2000

First Season: 1996

Baltimore lost its football team in 1984 when the Colts moved to Indianapolis. However, owner Art Modell brought the NFL back to Baltimore when he moved the Cleveland Browns there in 1996. The Ravens weren't allowed to keep the Browns' history, but they quickly made some of their own. The team developed one of the most dominant defenses the league had ever seen. Behind that strong defense, they won Super Bowl XXXV.

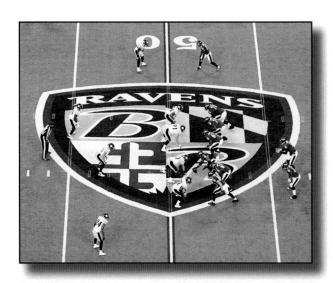

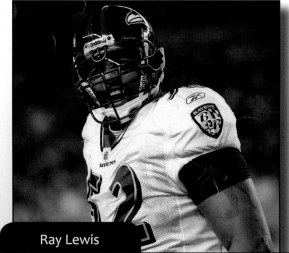

Ray Lewis

Peter Boulware	LB	1997–2007	Franchise's all-time leader in sacks with 70
Ray Lewis	LB	1996–present	Two-time Defensive Player of the Year and Super Bowl XXXV MVP
Jonathan Ogden	OT	1999–2006	Ravens' first draft pick was an 11-time Pro Bowl selection
Ed Reed	S	2002–present	Defensive Player of the Year in 2004

By the Numbers

TOP PASSER
Kyle Boller
2003–2007
7,846 yards

TOP RUSHER
Jamal Lewis
2000–2006
7,801 yards

TOP RECEIVER
Derrick Mason
2005–present
4,975 yards

MOST TDS SCORED
Jamal Lewis
47 TDs

Dominating Defense

In the year of their Super Bowl run, the Ravens defense was unstoppable. It allowed just 165 points during the regular season. The 10.3 points allowed per game was good for an NFL record for a 16-game season. That trend continued in the playoffs. Baltimore held its four opponents to just 23 total points. In the Ravens' 34-7 Super Bowl victory, the Giants' lone touchdown came on a kickoff return.

Super Bowl celebration

Quoth the Raven

The inspiration for the Ravens' nickname came from a famous poem, "The Raven," by Edgar Allan Poe. The writer lived in Baltimore for much of his life.

BUFFALO BILLS

First Season: 1960

Franchise Record: 354–394–8

Home Field: Ralph Wilson Stadium
(73,967 capacity) in Orchard Park, New York

CHAMPIONSHIPS
1964 (AFL), 1965 (AFL)

The Buffalo Bills started in the American Football League. They became one of the AFL's best teams, winning a pair of championships. They eventually became one of the best teams in the NFL too. They are the only team in history to play in four consecutive Super Bowls. Unfortunately for the Bills, they lost all four of the big games.

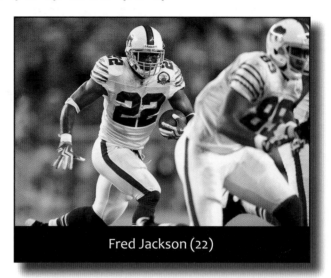
Fred Jackson (22)

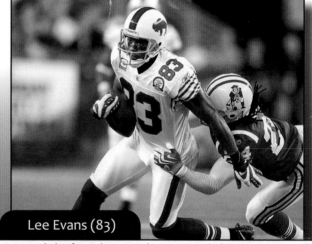
Lee Evans (83)

Lee Evans	WR	2004–present	First-round draft pick scored nine touchdowns as a rookie
Jim Kelly	QB	1986–1996	Led the Bills to four AFC championships
O.J. Simpson	RB	1969–1977	First back in NFL history to have a 2,000-yard season
Bruce Smith	DE	1985–1999	Dominant lineman set the NFL's all-time sack record with 200
Darryl Talley	LB	1983–1994	Bills' all-time leader in tackles
Thurman Thomas	RB	1988–1999	1991 MVP led the league in total yards four years in a row

By the Numbers

TOP PASSER	**Jim Kelly** 1986–1996 35,467 yards	
TOP RUSHER	**Thurman Thomas** 1988–1999 11,938 yards	
TOP RECEIVER	**Andre Reed** 1985–1999 13,095 yards	
MOST TDS SCORED	**Andre Reed and Thurman Thomas** 87 TDs each	

Comeback Kids

In the playoffs following the 1992 season, the Bills had the greatest comeback in NFL history. Buffalo was down 32 points in the third quarter and came back to tie the Houston Oilers. Kicker Steve Christie gave the Bills a 41-38 overtime victory with a 32-yard field goal.

Home Away from Home

Starting in 2008 the Bills played one regular-season game per season in Toronto, Ontario. Canada's largest city is just 90 miles (145 kilometers) from Buffalo, New York. The team considers it part of a large region of Bills fans.

CAROLINA PANTHERS

First Season: 1995

Franchise Record: 117–123–0
Home Field: Bank of America Stadium
(73,298 capacity) in Charlotte, North Carolina

CHAMPIONSHIPS
None

The Panthers wasted little time establishing themselves in the NFL. Founded in 1995, the team relied on defensive-minded head coaches Dom Capers and John Fox. Carolina went to two NFC championship games and one Super Bowl in its first 11 seasons.

DeShaun Foster extends for a touchdown in Super Bowl XXXVIII.

Legends & Stars

Julius Peppers (90)

Sam Mills	LB	1995–1997	Only Panthers player to be honored with a statue outside the stadium
Julius Peppers	DE	2002–2009	Athletic defensive end quickly became team's all-time sack leader
Steve Smith	WR	2001–present	Has had two 200-yard receiving games
Wesley Walls	TE	1996–2002	Five-time Pro Bowl selection scored 44 touchdowns for Carolina

By the Numbers

TOP PASSER
Jake Delhomme
2003–present
19,258 yards

TOP RUSHER
DeShaun Foster
2003–2007
3,336 yards

TOP RECEIVER
Muhsin Muhammad
1996–2004, 2008–present
9,255 yards

MOST TDS SCORED
Steve Smith
2001–present
58 TDs →

Defense Wins Championship

In 2001 the Panthers went a miserable 1–15. But they turned that around just two years later by making it to Super Bowl XXXVIII. To get to the big game, Carolina silenced the rowdy Philadelphia Eagles crowd in the NFC title game. Cornerback Ricky Manning Jr. had three interceptions, and the defense held the Eagles to a single field goal in a 14-3 win.

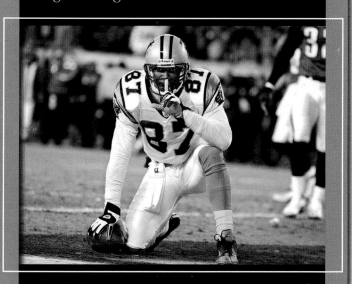

Muhsin Muhammad after a touchdown in the 2004 NFC title game

From Player to Owner

Panthers owner Jerry Richardson is the only NFL owner who played professional football. He played two seasons with the Baltimore Colts in 1959 and 1960.

CHICAGO BEARS

First Season: 1920

Franchise Record: 693–507–42
Home Field: Soldier Field
(61,500 capacity) in Chicago, Illinois

CHAMPIONSHIPS
1921, 1932, 1933, 1940, 1941, 1943, 1946, 1963, 1985

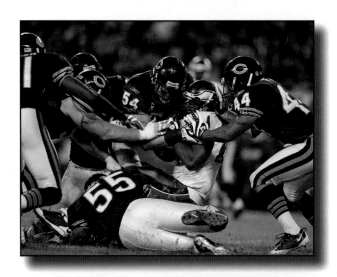

Known as the "Monsters of the Midway," the Chicago Bears are one of the oldest franchises in the NFL. They were founded by George "Papa Bear" Halas. He is known as the founder of professional football and one of the creators of the NFL. The Bears were born as the Decatur Staleys, but they moved to Chicago after one year.

Legends & Stars

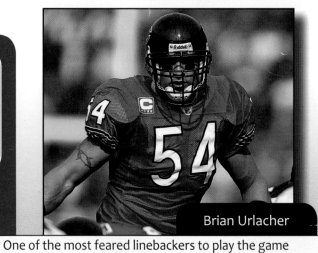

Brian Urlacher

Dick Butkus	LB	1965–1973	One of the most feared linebackers to play the game
Red Grange	RB	1925, 1929–1934	"The Galloping Ghost" was one of the NFL's first star players
George Halas		1920–1929, 1933–1942, 1946–1955, 1958–1967	Bears coach founded the team in 1920 and won 318 games, including six titles
Bronko Nagurski	FB	1930–1937, 1943	Four-time All-Pro could run and throw for scores
Walter Payton	RB	1975–1987	"Sweetness" held the all-time rushing record when he retired
Gale Sayers	RB	1965–1971	Electrifying and elusive runner could score from anywhere on the field
Mike Singletary	LB	1981–1992	Led one of the NFL's greatest defenses to a title in 1985
Brian Urlacher	LB	2000–present	Six-time Pro Bowl pick was Defensive Player of the Year in 2005

By the Numbers

TOP PASSER	**Sid Luckman** 1939–1950 14,686 yards	**TOP RUSHER** **Walter Payton** 1975–1987 16,726 yards →
TOP RECEIVER	**Johnny Morris** 1958–1967 5,059 yards	**MOST TDS SCORED** **Walter Payton** 125 TDs

Indoor Football

Long before teams started playing in domes, the Bears were forced to move inside to play for a championship. It was 1932, and a snowstorm made Chicago's Wrigley Field unplayable. So the Bears and the Portsmouth Spartans went into Chicago Stadium, an indoor sports arena. They played on an 80-yard field of dirt left over from a circus that had just left town. Fullback Bronko Nagurski led the Bears to a 9-0 win that day.

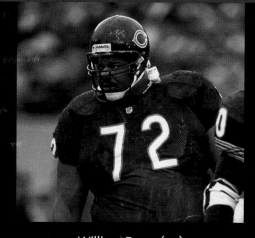

William Perry (72)

Check the Fridge

In 1985 the Bears won the Super Bowl behind a tough defense. But William "The Refrigerator" Perry, a 6-foot-2 (188-centimeter), 335-pound (152-kilogram) defensive lineman, played on offense too. He ran for two touchdowns and caught a touchdown pass that season. He also scored a touchdown in the Super Bowl.

CINCINNATI BENGALS

First Season: 1968

Franchise Record: 282–360–2

Home Field: Paul Brown Stadium
(65,535 capacity) in Cincinnati, Ohio

CHAMPIONSHIPS
None

With their distinctive tiger-striped helmets, the Cincinnati Bengals have always shown a little extra flare when they play. Running back Icky Woods danced the "Icky Shuffle." Wide receiver Chad Ochocinco is known for his bizarre touchdown celebrations. The team is also known for explosive quarterback play over the years, from Ken Anderson to Carson Palmer.

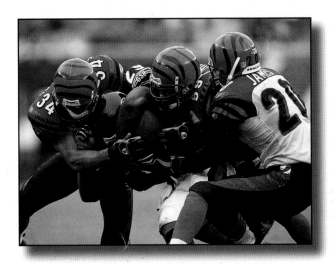

Legends & Stars

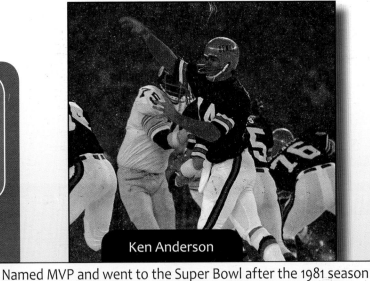

Ken Anderson

Ken Anderson	QB	1971–1986	Named MVP and went to the Super Bowl after the 1981 season
Boomer Esiason	QB	1984–1992, 1997	Led the Bengals to the 1998 AFC championship
Tim Krumrie	DT	1983–1994	Played in 188 games and was the team's all-time leading tackler
Anthony Munoz	OT	1980–1992	The only Bengals player elected to the Hall of Fame
Chad Ochocinco	WR	2001–present	Formerly known as Chad Johnson, Ochocinco has been named to six Pro Bowls

By the Numbers

TOP PASSER	**Ken Anderson** 1971–1986 32,838 yards	**TOP RUSHER**	**Corey Dillon** 1997–2003 8,061 yards
TOP RECEIVER	**Chad Ochocinco** 2001–present 9,952 yards	**MOST TDS SCORED**	**Pete Johnson** 1977–1983 70 TDs

Heartbreak City

The Bengals have often been called the Bungles because they've had so many losing seasons. But they have also been to two Super Bowls, falling both times to the mighty San Francisco 49ers. Cincinnati looked like it was on its way to win Super Bowl XXII in 1989. However, the 49ers' Joe Montana tossed a game-winning touchdown pass to John Taylor with 34 seconds left in the game.

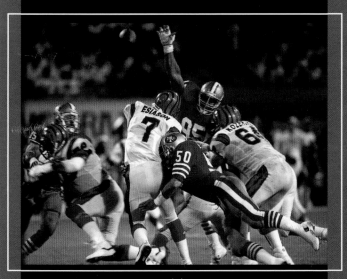

Boomer Esiason (7) under pressure during Super Bowl XXII

"Who Dey?"

Bengals fans often greet one another with the question, "Who dey?" The phrase goes back to the team's Super Bowl XVI run in 1982. The question is part of the longer chant, "Who dey think is going to beat them Bengals? Noooobody!"

CLEVELAND BROWNS

First Season: 1946

Franchise Record: 480–387–13
Home Field: Cleveland Browns Stadium
(73,200 capacity) in Cleveland, Ohio

CHAMPIONSHIPS
1946 (AAFC), 1947 (AAFC), 1948 (AAFC), 1949 (AAFC), 1950, 1954, 1955, 1964

Why would a team called the Browns have orange helmets? Because they're not named after the color, but after their founder and first coach, Paul Brown. The team's greatest player was also named Brown—Jim Brown—who is considered by many to be the greatest running back of all time.

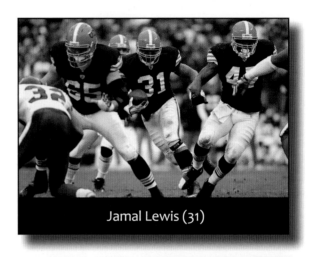
Jamal Lewis (31)

Legends & Stars

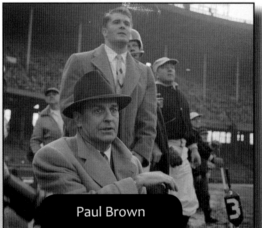
Paul Brown

Jim Brown	RB	1957–1965	Two-time MVP led the NFL in rushing eight times in nine seasons
Paul Brown		1946–1962	Browns coach won three NFL championships and had just one losing season in 17 years
Josh Cribbs	WR	2005–present	Pro Bowl pick scored four kinds of touchdowns in 2009—rushing, receiving, punt returning, and kick returning
Otto Graham	QB	1946–1955	Threw four touchdown passes in the 1950 title game and three in the 1954 game
Lou Groza	OT/K	1946–1959, 1961–1967	Kicked the game-winning field goal in the 1950 championship game
Marion Motley	RB	1946–1953	Once had 221 yards in a game on just 12 touches
Ozzie Newsome	TE	1978–1990	Set the NFL record for most catches by a tight end

By the Numbers

TOP PASSER	**Brian Sipe** 1974–1983 23,713 yards	**TOP RUSHER** **Jim Brown** 1957–1965 12,312 yards
TOP RECEIVER	**Ozzie Newsome** 1978–1990 7,980 yards	**MOST TDS SCORED** **Jim Brown** 126 TDs

Bursting onto the Scene

In their first four seasons, the Browns were members of the All-American Football Conference. The AAFC was a rival league to the NFL. When the AAFC folded, the Browns joined the NFL in 1950. They fit right in with their new league, appearing in six straight title games and winning three of them.

Cleveland Browns Stadium

Gone and Back

In 1996 the Browns moved to Baltimore and became the Ravens. However, the city of Cleveland got to keep the team's name and its history. Both were restored when the NFL brought pro football back to Cleveland in 1999.

DALLAS COWBOYS

First Season: 1960

Franchise Record: 434–314–6

Home Field: Cowboys Stadium
(80,000 capacity) in Arlington, Texas

CHAMPIONSHIPS
1971, 1977, 1992, 1993, 1995

If the NFL has a Hollywood team, it can be found deep in the heart of Texas. The Dallas Cowboys have always played with glitz and glam. Each player wears a big, blue star on the side of his silver helmet. The team's cheerleaders are the most famous in football. Most importantly, they know how to win. The Cowboys had 20 winning seasons in a row from 1966 to 1985. They also played in eight Super Bowls—more than any other team.

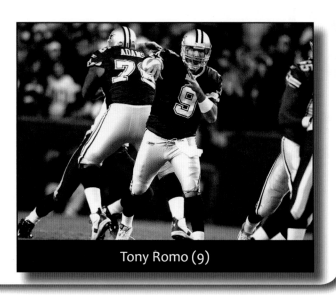
Tony Romo (9)

Legends & Stars

Troy Aikman

Troy Aikman	QB	1989–2000	Led the Cowboys to three Super Bowl wins
Tony Dorsett	RB	1977–1987	Once ran for a record 99-yard touchdown
Tom Landry		1960–1988	The Cowboys' head coach for their first 29 seasons
Bob Lilly	DT	1965–1974	"Mr. Cowboy" played in 11 Pro Bowls
Mel Renfro	CB	1964–1977	Selected to 10 consecutive Pro Bowls
Emmitt Smith	RB	1990–2002	NFL's all-time career rushing leader
Roger Staubach	QB	1969–1979	Played in four Super Bowls; MVP of Super Bowl VI
Jason Witten	TE	2003–present	Six-time Pro Bowler led the team in receptions four times

By the Numbers

TOP PASSER	**Troy Aikman** 1989–2000 32,942 yards	**TOP RUSHER**	**Emmitt Smith** 1990–2002 17,162 yards
TOP RECEIVER	**Michael Irvin** 1988–1999 11,904 yards	**MOST TDS SCORED**	**Emmitt Smith** 164 TDs

The Triplets

As good as the Cowboys were during their first 25 years, they did fall on hard times for a bit. But they returned to glory, thanks in part to three record-setting players. Quarterback Troy Aikman, running back Emmitt Smith, and wide receiver Michael Irvin helped the Cowboys get back on track. They were so good together—winning three Super Bowls in four years—that they were known as "The Triplets."

The Hat

The Cowboys' first coach didn't look like the men you see on the sidelines today. He didn't wear jackets with team logos or sweatshirts with the sleeves cut off. Tom Landry wore a jacket and tie and his famous fedora. The hat became the coach's symbol. When he was inducted into the Cowboys' Ring of Honor, an image of the hat was placed next to his name.

21

DENVER BRONCOS

Franchise Record: 394–352–10

Home Field: Invesco Field at Mile High
(76,125 capacity) in Denver, Colorado

CHAMPIONSHIPS
1997, 1998

First Season: 1960

When the American Football League was formed in 1960, a team was placed in the mile-high city of Denver, Colorado. The Broncos played in the league's first game and became its first winner, defeating the Boston Patriots. That winning continued long after the AFL and NFL merged, thanks to players such as quarterback John Elway, who led Denver to two championships.

John Elway hoisting the Lombardi Trophy after Super Bowl XXXII

Legends & Stars

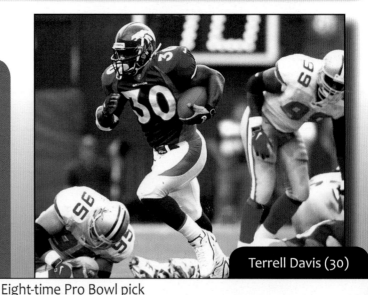

Terrell Davis (30)

Steve Atwater	S	1989–1998	Eight-time Pro Bowl pick
Terrell Davis	RB	1995–2001	Super Bowl MVP in 1997 and league MVP in 1998
John Elway	QB	1983–1998	1987 MVP played in five Super Bowls
Tom Jackson	LB	1973–1986	Played in 191 games over 14 seasons with Denver
Brandon Marshall	WR	2006–present	Pro Bowler caught a record 21 passes in a 2009 game
Gary Zimmerman	OT	1993–1997	Hall of Fame lineman was considered Elway's bodyguard

By the Numbers

TOP PASSER	**John Elway** 1983–1998 51,475 yards	
TOP RUSHER	**Terrell Davis** 1995–2001 7,607 yards	
TOP RECEIVER	**Rod Smith** 1995–2006 11,389 yards	
MOST TDS SCORED	**Rod Smith** 71 TDs	→

Losers to Winners

For many years, despite great success on the field, the Broncos were known for their losing ways. They played in Super Bowls XII, XXI, XXII, and XXIV. However, they came away as the runner-up each time. In Super Bowl XXXII, many thought they'd lose once again. Instead, John Elway and Terrell Davis led Denver to an upset win over the heavily favored Green Bay Packers. That win was the first of back-to-back Lombardi Trophy wins for the Broncos.

Terrell Davis (30) and Howard Griffith (29), Super Bowl XXXII

Orange Crush

Orange Crush is a tasty orange-flavored soda pop. But in the 1970s, it was also the nickname given to the dominating, orange-shirted, Denver Broncos defense. The tough defense was led by linebackers Randy Gradishar and Tom Jackson.

23

DETROIT LIONS

Franchise Record: 490–583–32
Home Field: Ford Field
(65,000 capacity) in Detroit Michigan

CHAMPIONSHIPS
1935, 1952, 1953, 1957

First Season: 1930

One of the greatest teams of the 1950s, the Lions are easily recognized by their silver and Honolulu blue uniforms. But they've fallen on hard times recently, winning only one playoff game since their 1957 title. In 2008 they became the only team in NFL history to go 0–16.

Calvin Johnson (81)

Legends & Stars

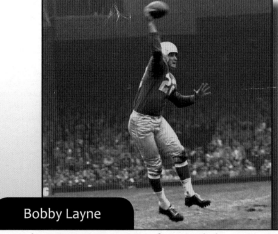

Bobby Layne

Lem Barney	CB	1967–1977	Returned seven interceptions for touchdowns in 11 seasons
Dick "Night Train" Lane	DB	1960–1965	Finished his career with 68 interceptions
Bobby Layne	QB	1950–1958	Two-minute-drill master led Lions to three titles
Barry Sanders	RB	1989–1998	Slippery and electric runner retired as the NFL's second all-time leading rusher
Matthew Stafford	QB	2009–present	No. 1 pick in the 2009 draft
Doak Walker	RB	1950–1955	Selected to five Pro Bowls in his six-year career

By the Numbers

TOP PASSER	**Bobby Layne** 1950–1958 15,710 yards	**TOP RUSHER**	**Barry Sanders** 1989–1998 15,269 yards	
TOP RECEIVER	**Herman Moore** 1991–2001 9,174 yards	**MOST TDS SCORED**	**Barry Sanders** 109 TDs →	

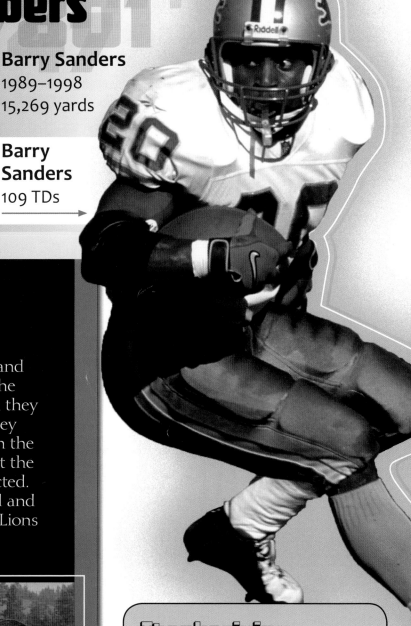

A Dominating Performance

In the early 1950s, the Lions and the Cleveland Browns were the best teams in the NFL. When they met in the 1957 title game, they had combined for five titles in the decade. But the game was not the tough match most had expected. Detroit opened up a 31-7 lead and went on to win 59-14. Seven Lions scored touchdowns that day.

Doak Walker (37), Bobby Layne (22), and coach Buddy Parker

Thanksgiving Tradition

It wouldn't be Thanksgiving Day without turkey, pumpkin pie, and the Detroit Lions. Almost every year since 1934, the Lions have played a home game on Thanksgiving. Their record on that day is 33–35–2.

25

GREEN BAY PACKERS

Franchise Record: 654–518–36

Home Field: Lambeau Field
(72,601 capacity) in Green Bay, Wisconsin

CHAMPIONSHIPS
1929, 1930, 1931, 1936, 1939, 1944,
1961, 1962, 1965, 1966, 1967, 1996

First Season: 1919

From Curly Lambeau in 1919 to Aaron Rodgers in 2009, football players have dominated the gridiron in Green Bay, Wisconsin, for more than 90 years. With 12 championships, including the first two Super Bowls, the Packers have more titles than any other franchise in league history.

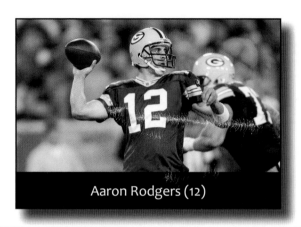

Aaron Rodgers (12)

Legends & Stars

Reggie White

Brett Favre	QB	1992–2007	Three-time MVP and NFL's all-time leader in passing yards and touchdowns
Don Hutson	WR	1935–1945	Considered the NFL's first star receiver
Vince Lombardi		1959–1969	Packers coach won five championships in nine seasons, including Super Bowls I and II after the 1966 and 1967 seasons
Ray Nitchke	LB	1958–1972	Hall of Famer had 25 interceptions and 23 fumble recoveries in 15 seasons
Bart Starr	QB	1956–1971	Led the Packers to five championships and was MVP of Super Bowls I and II
Reggie White	DE	1993–1998	Sack master helped Green Bay win Super Bowl XXXI
Charles Woodson	CB	2006–present	Defensive Player of the Year in 2009

By the Numbers

TOP PASSER	**Brett Favre** 1992–2007 61,655 yards	**TOP RUSHER**	**Ahman Green** 2000–2006, 2009 8,251 yards	
TOP RECEIVER	**James Lofton** 1978–1986 9,656 yards	**MOST TDS SCORED**	**Don Hutson** 1935–1945 105 TDs	

The Ice Bowl

The temperature was a bone-chilling minus 13 degrees Fahrenheit (minus 25 degrees Celsius), and Lambeau Field was a sheet of ice. That day in 1967, the Packers and the Cowboys played for the NFL title and a spot in Super Bowl II. Bart Starr's quarterback sneak with 16 seconds to go gave the Packers a 21-17 victory in what is now called "The Ice Bowl."

The Fans Own the Team

The Packers are the only NFL franchise without an owner. The team is publicly owned with 112,120 stockholders around the country each owning a small piece of the Pack.

Packers fans wearing cheesehead hats

HOUSTON TEXANS

First Season: 2002

Franchise Record: 49–79–0

Home Field: Reliant Stadium
(69,500 capacity) in Houston, Texas

CHAMPIONSHIPS
None

Texas is football country, but the state's largest city lost an NFL team in 1997. That year Houston's beloved Oilers moved to Tennessee and later became the Titans. However, in 2002 the city was given a second chance, and the Houston Texans were born. They quickly won over fans with a victory in their very first game. That day they defeated the Dallas Cowboys 19-10.

Andre Johnson

Andre Johnson	WR	2003–present	Three-time Pro Bowler led the NFL in receptions twice
Matt Schaub	QB	2007–present	Led franchise to its first winning record in 2009
Mario Williams	DE	2006–present	Pro Bowl pick has racked up 39.5 sacks in his first four seasons

By the Numbers

TOP PASSER	**David Carr** 2002–2006 13,391 yards	**TOP RUSHER**	**Domanick Williams** 2003–2005 3,195 yards	
TOP RECEIVER	**Andre Johnson** 2003–present 7,948 yards	**MOST TDS SCORED**	**Andre Johnson** 42 TDs	

Big Foot

The Texans' top point scorer, kicker Kris Brown, had a historic day in 2007. He not only kicked five field goals, but he also became the first player in NFL history to make three field goals of 54 yards or longer. He hit from 54 yards twice. Then he won the game against the Miami Dolphins with a 57-yarder with one second left on the clock.

Draft Day Shocker

The Texans had the No. 1 draft pick in 2006. Many people thought they would take electrifying running back Reggie Bush. The night before the draft, Houston surprised everyone by signing defensive end Mario Williams to a contract. The move paid off—Williams has already made himself the team's all-time sack leader.

29

INDIANAPOLIS COLTS

First Season: 1953

Franchise Record: 441–390–7
Home Field: Lucas Oil Stadium
(63,000 capacity) in Indianapolis, Indiana

CHAMPIONSHIPS
1958, 1959, 1970, 2006

The Colts have always been one of the NFL's greatest teams. They excelled outdoors in Baltimore for 31 years, and they kept it going under a dome in Indianapolis. They have also had two of the greatest quarterbacks to ever play the game. Johnny Unitas led the way in the 1950s and 1960s. In the late 1990s and 2000s, it was Peyton Manning who returned the franchise to glory.

Peyton Manning, Super Bowl XLI

Legends & Stars

Reggie Wayne (87)

Raymond Berry	WR	1955–1967	Caught 12 passes for 178 yards in the 1958 title game
Peyton Manning	QB	1998–present	Four-time NFL MVP
Gino Marchetti	DE	1953–1966	One of the greatest defensive ends in NFL history
Lenny Moore	RB	1956–1967	Scored touchdowns in 18 consecutive games
Jim Parker	OL	1957–1967	First full-time offensive lineman elected to the Hall of Fame
Johnny Unitas	QB	1956–1972	Retired as the NFL's all-time leader in most passing categories
Reggie Wayne	WR	2001–present	Four-time Pro Bowl pick

By the Numbers

TOP PASSER	**Peyton Manning** 1998–present 50,128 yards	TOP RUSHER	**Edgerrin James** 1999–2005 9,226 yards
TOP RECEIVER	**Marvin Harrison** 1996–2008 14,580 yards	MOST TDS SCORED	**Marvin Harrison** 128 TDs

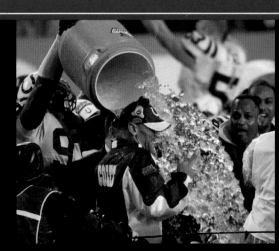

The Greatest Game?

Even though it was more than a half a century ago, the 1958 NFL championship game is still remembered as one of the best. It was also one of the first games to be broadcast on national TV. There were 15 future Hall of Famers on the muddy field that day. Johnny Unitas and Alan Ameche led Baltimore to a 23-17 overtime victory over the New York Giants.

Historic Title

When the Colts won Super Bowl XLI, NFL history was made. With the victory, Tony Dungy became the first African-American coach to win a Super Bowl. Dungy coached the Colts for seven seasons and never had a losing record.

Tony Dungy (center), Super Bowl XLI

JACKSONVILLE JAGUARS

Franchise Record: 125–115–0

Home Field:
Jacksonville Municipal Stadium
(67,164 capacity) in Jacksonville, Florida

CHAMPIONSHIPS
None

First Season: 1995

Jacksonville, Florida, is located deep in the heart of college football country. It's where the University of Florida and the University of Georgia renew their rivalry every year. It's also where the Gator Bowl is played. But when the NFL expanded in 1995, it finally gave fans in that area the professional version of its game, and the Jaguars were born.

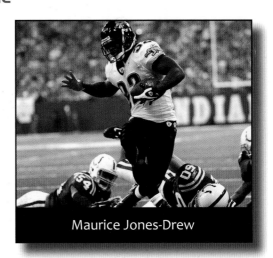
Maurice Jones-Drew

Legends & Stars

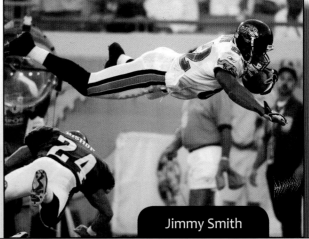
Jimmy Smith

Tony Boselli	OT	1995–2001	Five-time Pro Bowl pick
Mark Brunell	QB	1995–2003	Threw 144 touchdown passes for the Jags
Maurice Jones-Drew	RB	2006–present	Versatile back named to Pro Bowl in 2009
Jimmy Smith	WR	1995–2005	Led the NFL with 116 catches in 1999

By the Numbers

TOP PASSER	**Mark Brunell** 1995–2003 25,698 yards	**TOP RUSHER**	**Fred Taylor** 1998–2008 11,271 yards
TOP RECEIVER	**Jimmy Smith** 1995–2005 12,287 yards	**MOST TDS SCORED**	**Fred Taylor** 70 TDs

Fitting Right In

In just their second season as a franchise, the Jaguars shocked everyone and found themselves one game away from the Super Bowl. Led by running back Natrone Means and quarterback Mark Brunell, Jacksonville won seven games in a row, including a stunning 30-27 second-round playoff victory over the favored Denver Broncos. Their impressive streak ended when they lost 20-6 to the New England Patriots in the 1996 AFC championship game.

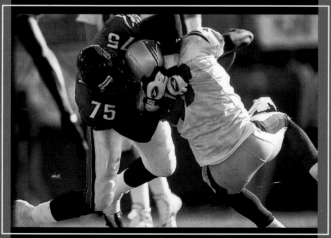

The Jaguars got revenge on the Patriots, winning 25-10 in a 1999 AFC Wild Card playoff game.

Piling on Points

Following the 1999 season, retiring Miami Dolphins great Dan Marino ended his career on a sour note with a 62-7 playoff loss to the Jaguars. It was the most points ever scored in an AFC playoff game and second-most in NFL postseason history.

KANSAS CITY CHIEFS

First Season: 1960

Franchise Record: 385–359–12

Home Field: Arrowhead Stadium
(79,451 capacity) in Kansas City, Missouri

CHAMPIONSHIPS
1962 (AFL), 1966 (AFL), 1969

The Kansas City Chiefs started out in Dallas as the AFL's Texans. Then-owner Lamar Hunt wanted his own team to rival the NFL's newest team, the Cowboys. After three years, Hunt moved his team north and changed its name to the Chiefs. The team was a powerhouse in the AFL and became a champion in the NFL as well.

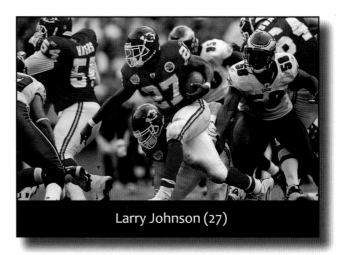

Larry Johnson (27)

Legends & Stars

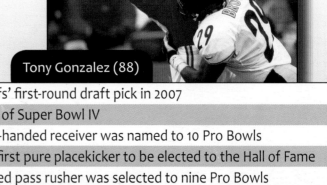

Tony Gonzalez (88)

Dwayne Bowe	WR	2007–present	Chiefs' first-round draft pick in 2007
Len Dawson	QB	1962–1975	MVP of Super Bowl IV
Tony Gonzalez	TE	1997–2008	Sure-handed receiver was named to 10 Pro Bowls
Jan Stenerud	K	1967–1979	The first pure placekicker to be elected to the Hall of Fame
Derrick Thomas	LB	1989–1999	Feared pass rusher was selected to nine Pro Bowls
Emmitt Thomas	CB	1966–1978	Five-time Pro Bowler had 58 interceptions

By the Numbers

TOP PASSER
Len Dawson
1962–1975
28,507 yards

TOP RUSHER
Priest Holmes
2001–2007
6,070 yards

TOP RECEIVER
Tony Gonzalez
1997–2008
10,940 yards

MOST TDS SCORED
Priest Holmes
83 TDs

Super Team

In the first four years of the Super Bowl era, the big game was played between the champions of the NFL and the AFL. The Chiefs played in two of those games. First they fell to the mighty Green Bay Packers in Super Bowl I in 1967. The next time they upset the Minnesota Vikings in Super Bowl IV, giving the AFL the last laugh before its teams merged with the NFL later in 1970.

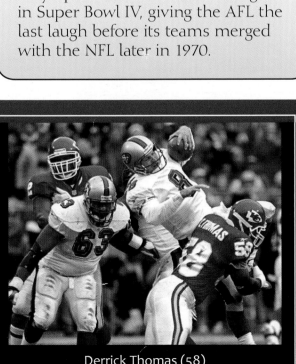

Derrick Thomas (58)

Sack Attack

In 1990 Chiefs great Derrick Thomas (58) led the NFL with 20 sacks. The linebacker picked up more than a third of those sacks in a single game. He had a league-record seven sacks against the Seattle Seahawks.

MIAMI DOLPHINS

First Season: 1966

Franchise Record: 387–281–4

Home Field: Sun Life Stadium
(76,500 capacity) in Miami Gardens, Florida

CHAMPIONSHIPS
1972, 1973

Fans of the Miami Dolphins have been lucky, and not just because of the beautiful Florida weather. Their favorite team has gone to five Super Bowls and won two championships. The team also celebrated an undefeated season. The Dolphins have been led by one of the game's greatest coaches, as well as one of its greatest quarterbacks.

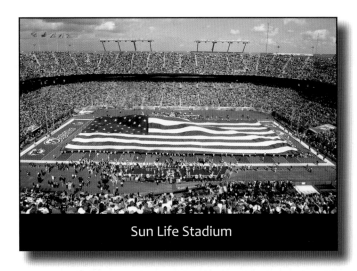
Sun Life Stadium

Legends & Stars

Larry Csonka (39)

Ronnie Brown	RB	2005–present	Pro Bowl back helped popularize the wildcat offense
Larry Csonka	RB	1968–1979	MVP of Super Bowl VIII
Bob Griese	QB	1967–1980	Led the Dolphins to three AFC titles and two Super Bowl wins
Jim Langer	C	1970–1979	Played every offensive down during the 1972 season
Larry Little	G	1969–1980	Five-time Pro Bowl pick
Dan Marino	QB	1983–1999	Played 17 seasons and was the NFL's all-time passing leader when he retired in 1999
Don Shula		1970–1995	Dolphins coach won two Super Bowls in 26 seasons with Miami

By the Numbers

TOP PASSER	**Dan Marino** 1983–1999 61,361 yards	**TOP RUSHER**	**Larry Csonka** 1968–1979 6,737 yards
TOP RECEIVER	**Mark Duper** 1982–1992 8,869 yards	**MOST TDS SCORED**	**Mark Clayton** 1983–1992 82 TDs

The Perfect Season

Each season, when the last undefeated NFL team finally loses a game, a few members of the 1972 Miami Dolphins get together to celebrate. That's because the 1972 Dolphins team was the last to go through a season and the playoffs without losing. The Dolphins went 14–0 during the regular season and 3–0 in the playoffs. They beat the Washington Redskins 14-7 in Super Bowl VII.

Don Shula (center) and the 1972 Dolphins at a halftime ceremony in 2007

Winning Ways

Don Shula coached in the NFL for 33 seasons. He started with the Baltimore Colts and then went to the Dolphins. He won more games (347) than any other coach. He had only two losing seasons.

MINNESOTA VIKINGS

First Season: 1961

Franchise Record: 407–326–9
Home Field:
Hubert H. Humphrey Metrodome
(63,669 capacity) in Minneapolis, Minnesota

CHAMPIONSHIPS
None

The Minnesota Vikings have always made opposing teams nervous. The "Purple People Eaters" stuffed offenses in chilly Metropolitan Stadium in the 1960s and 1970s. Randy Moss and Adrian Peterson sprinted away from defenses in the Metrodome in the 2000s. Although they've never won a title, the Vikings have reached the Super Bowl four times.

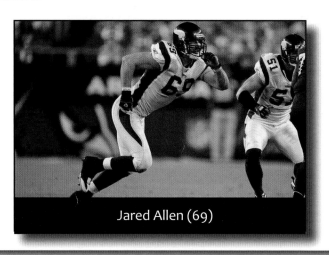
Jared Allen (69)

Legends & Stars

Fran Tarkenton

Carl Eller	DE	1964–1978	Fearsome sack master played in six Pro Bowls
Jim Marshall	DE	1961–1979	Played in 282 consecutive games
Randy Moss	WR	1998–2004	Shattered NFL rookie record by catching 17 touchdown passes in a single season
Alan Page	DT	1967–1978	The 1971 MVP had 173 career sacks and blocked 28 kicks
Adrian Peterson	RB	2007–present	Pro Bowler scored 40 touchdowns in his first three seasons
Fran Tarkenton	QB	1961–1966, 1972–1978	Was NFL's all-time passing leader when he retired

By the Numbers

Running Free

It didn't take long for running back Adrian Peterson to burst onto the NFL scene. Just eight games into his 2007 rookie season, Peterson set the league's single-game rushing record. He ran 296 yards in a 35-17 win over the San Diego Chargers. He put himself in the company of other great Vikings backs such as Robert Smith, Chuck Foreman, and Bill Brown.

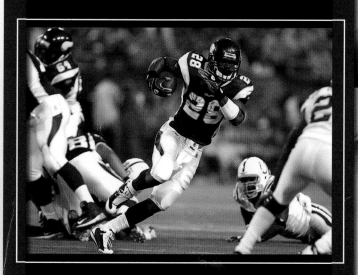

Adrian Peterson (28)

Purple Pride

Defensive linemen Alan Page, Carl Eller, Jim Marshall, and Gary Larsen were called the "Purple People Eaters." The purple-clad defensive line got the nickname from a popular song of the same name.

NEW ENGLAND PATRIOTS

Franchise Record: 387–360–9
Home Field: Gillette Stadium
(68,756 capacity) in Foxborough, Massachussetts

CHAMPIONSHIPS
2001, 2003, 2004

First Season: 1960

They started as the Boston Patriots when the American Football League was created in 1960. Later they moved south a few miles and were claimed by all of New England. By the 2000s the Patriots had become a football dynasty. They won three Super Bowls in a span of four years. They also became the first NFL team to go 16–0 in the regular season.

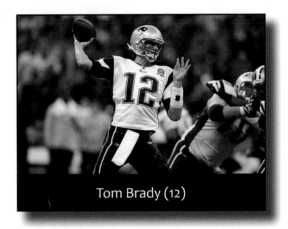
Tom Brady (12)

Legends & Stars

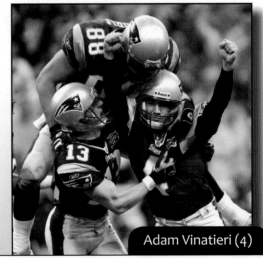
Adam Vinatieri (4)

Bill Belichick		2000–present	Patriots coach led New England to three championships
Tom Brady	QB	2001–present	Two-time Super Bowl MVP holds the single-season touchdown pass record (50)
John Hannah	G	1973–1985	Selected to nine Pro Bowls
Mike Haynes	CB	1976–1982	Nine-time Pro Bowler had 46 career interceptions
Andre Tippett	LB	1982–1993	One of the top sack masters of the 1980s
Adam Vinatieri	K	1996–2005	Nailed last-second, game-winning field goals in Super Bowls XXXVI and XXXVIII
Wes Welker	WR	2007–present	Brady's go-to guy for three years, catching more than 100 passes per season

By the Numbers

TOP PASSER	**Drew Bledsoe** 1993–2001 29,657 yards	**TOP RUSHER**	**Sam Cunningham** 1973–1982 5,453 yards
TOP RECEIVER	**Stanley Morgan** 1977–1989 10,352 yards	**MOST TDS SCORED**	**Stanley Morgan** 68 TDs

Team First

Everyone figured the Patriots would lose when they faced the St. Louis Rams in Super Bowl XXXVI. Everyone except the Patriots, that is. Before the game no individuals were introduced to the New Orleans Superdome crowd. Instead, the Pats ran onto the field together. In the game's final seconds, kicker Adam Vinatieri made a 48-yard field goal to give his team a stunning 20-17 win.

The Patriots celebrate Adam Vinatieri's game-winning field goal in Super Bowl XXXVI.

The Snowplow Game

One of the craziest moments in NFL history occurred on a snowy day in 1982. Late in the game, a worker at New England's Schaefer Stadium drove a tractor onto the snowy field. He cleared a spot for John Smith to kick the winning field goal in a 3-0 win over the Miami Dolphins.

NEW ORLEANS SAINTS

Franchise Record: 275–378–5

Home Field: Louisiana Superdome (72,000 capacity) in New Orleans, Louisiana

CHAMPIONSHIP
2009

First Season: 1967

The Saints didn't exactly "come marching in" to the NFL. It took 13 years before they had a .500 season and another eight seasons before they made the playoffs. But then things began to turn around. The Saints started winning games behind a dominating defense led by Sam Mills in the '80s and '90s. In the 2000s Drew Brees brought a high-powered offense to New Orleans and eventually led the Saints to a stunning Super Bowl victory.

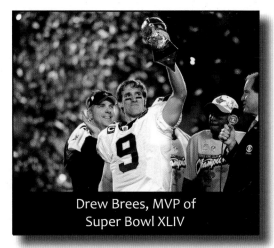

Drew Brees, MVP of Super Bowl XLIV

Legends & Stars

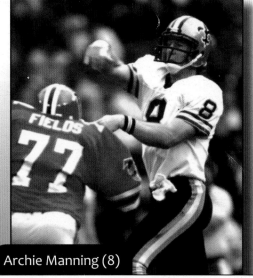

Archie Manning (8)

Morten Anderson	K	1982–1994	NFL's all-time points leader spent half of his career with the Saints
Drew Brees	QB	2006–present	Four-time Pro Bowl selection and MVP of Super Bowl XLIV
Rickey Jackson	LB	1981–1993	Finished career as the team's all-time leading tackler in 13 seasons
Archie Manning	QB	1971–1982	Tossed 125 career touchdown passes; father of quarterbacks Peyton and Eli Manning
Willie Roaf	OT	1993–2001	11-time Pro Bowl selection, including seven times with the Saints

By the Numbers

Super Home

In 2005 Hurricane Katrina devastated the city of New Orleans, Louisiana. The destruction forced the Saints to move out of the Superdome for one season. After returning to their home, the Saints set out to do something special for the city and their loyal fans. In 2009 the Saints did just that. They upset the powerful Indianapolis Colts 31-17 in Super Bowl XLIV. The Saints trailed 10-0 before rallying behind two second-half touchdown passes by Drew Brees.

The Saints take the field for their first game back in the Superdome in 2006.

What a Kick!

Saints kicker Tom Dempsey was born without toes on his right foot and wore a special shoe. In 1970 he kicked a 63-yard field goal—an NFL record.

43

NEW YORK GIANTS

Franchise Record: 626–518–33

Home Field: New Meadowlands Stadium (82,500 capacity) in East Rutherford, New Jersey

CHAMPIONSHIPS
1927, 1934, 1938, 1956, 1986, 1990, 2007

First Season: 1925

Only four of the 20 professional teams that existed in 1925 are still around today. The New York Giants is one of them, and the team has given nearly every generation of fans the thrill of a championship. Fullback Jack McBride led the way to a title in 1927. Eighty years later quarterback Eli Manning held the Lombardi Trophy as a Super Bowl winner.

Eli Manning hoists the Lombardi Trophy after Super Bowl XLII.

Legends & Stars

Lawrence Taylor (56)

Frank Gifford	HB/DB	1953–1964	Played offense, defense, and special teams in the 1950s and 1960s
Mel Hein	C	1931–1945	Named the league's MVP in 1938
Sam Huff	LB	1956–1963	One of the league's first defensive stars; played in five Pro Bowls
Eli Manning	QB	2004–present	Led the Giants to Super Bowl XLII win
Bill Parcells		1983–1990	Giants coach led New York to championships in Super Bowl XXI and XXV
Lawrence Taylor	LB	1981–1993	Dominating defensive force was named to 10 Pro Bowls
Y.A. Tittle	QB	1961–1964	League MVP in 1961 and 1963

By the Numbers

What a Catch!

The Giants upset the New England Patriots to win Super Bowl XLII with a late touchdown. The game-winning drive was kept alive by an amazing catch by little-used receiver David Tyree. As he fell to the turf, Tyree had to pin the ball to his helmet to keep the pass from falling incomplete. Four plays later the Giants scored the go-ahead touchdown.

A Big Splash

Big victories are often celebrated with players dumping Gatorade on their coaches. Credit Hall of Fame Giants linebacker Harry Carson for starting it all. He splashed coach Bill Parcells after each victory on the way to the 1986 championship.

45

NEW YORK JETS

First Season: 1960

Franchise Record: 340–408–8
Home Field: New Meadowlands Stadium
(82,500 capacity) in East Rutherford, New Jersey

CHAMPIONSHIPS
1968

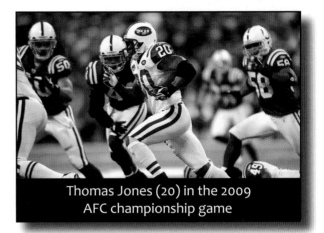

Thomas Jones (20) in the 2009
AFC championship game

The New York Jets were born in the American Football League in 1960. For their first three seasons, however, they were known as the New York Titans. The name was similar to their NFL counterpart in the Big Apple, the New York Giants. Not only did the team change its name, but it changed its colors, and "Gang Green" was born.

Legends & Stars

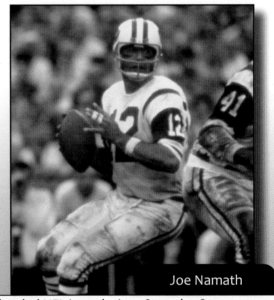

Joe Namath

Mark Gastineau	DE	1979–1988	Speed rusher led NFL in sacks in 1983 and 1984
Joe Klecko	DL	1977–1987	Part of the "New York Sack Exchange" with Gastineau
Curtis Martin	RB	1998–2005	Fourth on the NFL's all-time rushing list
Don Maynard	WR	1960–1972	Four-time Pro Bowl pick
Joe Namath	QB	1965–1976	MVP of Super Bowl III
Darrelle Revis	CB	2007–present	"Shut-down" corner named to two Pro Bowls
Mark Sanchez	QB	2009–present	First-round pick took Jets to the AFC title game as a rookie

By the Numbers

TOP PASSER	**Joe Namath** 1965–1976 27,057 yards	
TOP RUSHER	**Curtis Martin** → 1998–2005 10,302 yards	
TOP RECEIVER	**Don Maynard** 1960–1972 11,732 yards	
MOST TDS SCORED	**Don Maynard** 88 TDs	

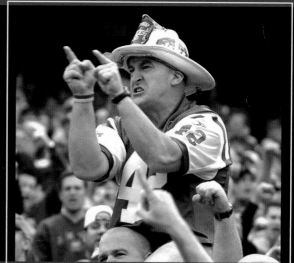

Broadway Joe's Guarantee

When the Jets played the Baltimore Colts in Super Bowl III, the game still pitted the winner of the American Football League against the winner of the National Football League. Many people considered the NFL to be much better than the AFL and didn't give New York a chance. Three days before the big game, Jets quarterback Joe Namath guaranteed that his team would win. Sure enough, Namath and the Jets ran off the field with a shocking 16-7 victory.

A Fiery Fan

Not many fans stick out among the tens of thousands of people who sit in stadiums each Sunday. But Ed Anzalone does. Known as Fireman Ed, the New York City firefighter wears a green-and-white fireman's hat. He is known for leading the crowd in their famous cheer, "J-E-T-S! Jets! Jets! Jets!"

OAKLAND RAIDERS

Franchise Record: 410–335–11

Home Field: Oakland-Alameda County Coliseum (63,026 capacity) in Oakland, California

CHAMPIONSHIPS
1967 (AFL), 1976, 1980, 1983

First Season: 1960

The Raiders have built a reputation as one of the most intimidating teams in pro football history. The team is known for its silver and black colors, its pirate logo, and its "Black Hole" of crazed and costumed fans at one end of their home stadium. But the players have given fans much to cheer about too. The Raiders have won four championships and played in five Super Bowls.

Legends & Stars

Marcus Allen

Marcus Allen	RB	1982–1992	Super Bowl XVIII MVP and league MVP in 1985
Nnamdi Asomugha	CB	2003–present	Two-time Pro Bowl pick
Fred Biletnikoff	WR	1965–1978	Caught at least 40 passes in 10 consecutive seasons
George Blanda	QB/K	1967–1975	Played 26 seasons of pro football, more than any other player
Howie Long	DE	1981–1993	Pass rusher was an eight-time Pro Bowl pick
John Madden		1969–1978	Raiders coach never had a losing record; he led the Raiders to a Super Bowl XI victory
Jim Otto	C	1960–1974	Started at center for the Raiders' first 15 seasons

By the Numbers

TOP PASSER	**Ken Stabler** 1970–1979 19,078 yards	**TOP RUSHER**	**Marcus Allen** 1982–1992 8,545 yards	
TOP RECEIVER	**Tim Brown** 1988–2003 4,734 yards	**MOST TDS SCORED**	**Tim Brown** 104 TDs	

Coining a Phrase

Raiders owner Al Davis coached the team in its early years. He is famous for his mottos, "Commitment to excellence" and "Just win, baby," among others. His Raiders have followed through too. During a stretch of 20 years from the mid-1960s to the mid-1980s, the Raiders had 19 winning seasons.

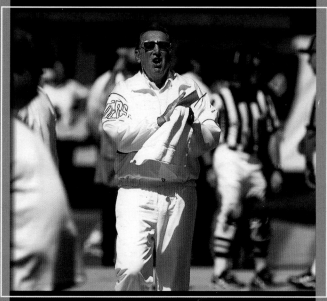

To L.A. and Back

Oakland may be the Raiders' home, but for 12 seasons they were all Hollywood. From 1982 to 1994, they played in Los Angeles. They won Super Bowl XVIII as the Los Angeles Raiders.

PHILADELPHIA EAGLES

Franchise Record: 499–535–26

Home Field: Lincoln Financial Field
(68,532 capacity) in Philadelphia, Pennsylvania

CHAMPIONSHIPS
1948, 1949, 1960

First Season: 1933

Philadelphia is often called the "City of Brotherly Love." However, the Eagles haven't shown much love for their opponents over their nearly 80-year history. Chuck Bednarik was a fierce competitor on both sides of the ball in the early years. Later the Eagles featured such double-threat (passing and running) quarterbacks as Randall Cunningham and Donovan McNabb, making life miserable for opposing defenses.

Legends & Stars

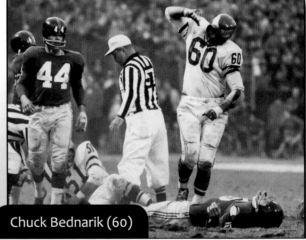

Chuck Bednarik (60)

Chuck Bednarik	C/LB	1949–1962	Played both offense and defense, yet missed only three games in 14 years
Randall Cunningham	QB	1985–1995	NFL's all-time quarterback rushing leader
Ron Jaworski	QB	1977–1986	Led the Eagles to their first Super Bowl game
Donovan McNabb	QB	1999–2009	Five-time Pro Bowl selection
Norm Van Brocklin	QB	1958–1960	1960 MVP led the Eagles to their last championship
Steve Van Buren	HB	1944–1951	Led NFL in rushing four times in the 1940s

By the Numbers

TOP PASSER	**Donovan McNabb** 1999–2009 32,873 yards	**TOP RUSHER**	**Wilbert Montgomery** 1977–1984 6,538 yards
TOP RECEIVER	**Harold Carmichael** 1972–1983 8,978 yards	**MOST TDS SCORED**	**Harold Carmichael** 79 TDs

Duffel Bag Dynasty

In the late 1940s, many of the Philadelphia Eagles joined the team shortly after fighting in World War II. They came together to win back-to-back NFL championships in 1948 and 1949, shutting out their opponents in both games. They defeated the Chicago Cardinals 7-0 and the Los Angeles Rams 14-0.

Dominant Decade

In the 2000s the Eagles went to five NFC championship games. Led by coach Andy Reid and quarterback Donovan McNabb (5), that stretch included four title games in a row and a win after the 2004 season to get to Super Bowl XXXIX.

PITTSBURGH STEELERS

Franchise Record: 529–495–20
Home Field: Heinz Field
(65,050 capacity) in Pittsburgh, Pennsylvania

CHAMPIONSHIPS
1974, 1975, 1978, 1979, 2005, 2008

First Season: 1933

Only four teams in the NFL are older than the Pittsburgh Steelers. But in the Super Bowl era, no team has won more championships. Before winning their fifth Super Bowl after the 2005 season, the Steelers' cry was, "Win one for the thumb." They already had a championship ring for each finger on one hand. Three years later Pittsburgh won its sixth Lombardi Trophy and "one for the other thumb."

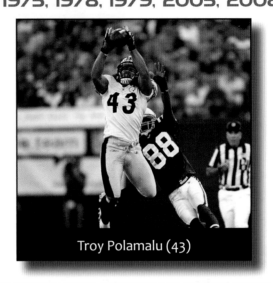
Troy Polamalu (43)

Jerome Bettis

Legends & Stars

Jerome Bettis	RB	1996–2005	"The Bus" went to six Pro Bowls
Terry Bradshaw	QB	1970–1983	Won four Super Bowls and was MVP of two of them
"Mean" Joe Greene	DT	1969–1981	10-time Pro Bowler and two-time Defensive Player of the Year
James Harrison	LB	2002–present	Had a 100-yard interception return for a touchdown in Super Bowl XLIII
Jack Lambert	LB	1974–1984	The leader of Pittsburgh's "Steel Curtain" defense
Chuck Noll		1969–1991	Steelers coach spent 23 seasons in Pittsburgh and won four Super Bowls in the 1970s
Ben Roethlisberger	QB	2004–present	Won two Super Bowls in his first five seasons
John Stallworth	WR	1974–1987	Caught the winning touchdown pass in Super Bowl XIV

By the Numbers

TOP PASSER	**Terry Bradshaw** 1970–1983 27,989 yards	**TOP RUSHER**	**Franco Harris** 1972–1983 11,950 yards
TOP RECEIVER	**Hines Ward** 1999–present 10,947 yards	**MOST TDS SCORED**	**Franco Harris** 100 TDs

The Immaculate Reception

The Steelers made one of the wildest plays in football history in a 1972 playoff game. Pittsburgh trailed by one point in the game's final minute. Terry Bradshaw tried to pass to John Fuqua on fourth down. The pass was broken up by a defender, but the ball deflected backward to Franco Harris, who scooped it up and raced 42 yards for the winning touchdown.

Great Hands

Wide receivers led the way in three of the Steelers' Super Bowl victories and won game MVP awards. Lynn Swann had four catches for 161 yards and a touchdown in Super Bowl X. Hines Ward had five catches for 123 yards and a touchdown in Super Bowl XL. Santonio Holmes had nine catches for 131 yards and the game-winning touchdown in Super Bowl XLIII.

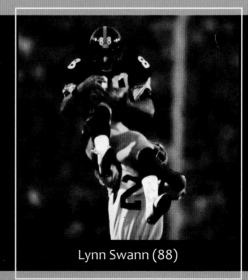

Lynn Swann (88)

53

SAN DIEGO CHARGERS

First Season: 1960

Franchise Record: 375–370–11

Home Field: Qualcomm Stadium
(71,294 capacity) in San Diego, California

CHAMPIONSHIPS
1963 (AFL)

Like the lightning bolt flashing on their helmets, the Chargers have always had an electrifying offense. In the early days, wide receiver Lance Alworth caught touchdown passes. Quarterback Dan Fouts threw them in the 1970s and 1980s. And running back LaDainian Tomlinson ran in scores in more recent years. No matter how they did it, the Chargers could always put points on the scoreboard.

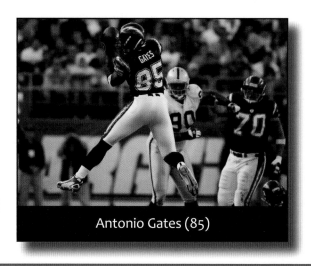
Antonio Gates (85)

Legends & Stars

Junior Seau (55)

Lance Alworth	F/WR	1962–1970	First AFL star to be inducted into the Hall of Fame
Dan Fouts	QB	1973–1987	Led the NFL in passing for four consecutive seasons
Charlie Joiner	WR	1976–1986	Played more games than any other receiver at the time of his retirement
Philip Rivers	QB	2004–present	Two-time Pro Bowl selection
Junior Seau	LB	1990–2002	Chargers top tackler was selected to 12 Pro Bowls
LaDainian Tomlinson	RB	2001–2009	NFL MVP in 2006

By the Numbers

TOP PASSER
Dan Fouts
1973–1987
43,040 yards

TOP RUSHER
LaDainian Tomlinson
2001–2009
12,490 yards

TOP RECEIVER
Lance Alworth
1962–1970
9,584 yards

MOST TDS SCORED
LaDainian Tomlinson
153 TDs

Air Coryell

Coach Don Coryell's offense was so potent that it quickly got the nickname "Air Coryell." It was driven by the arm of quarterback Dan Fouts and the hands of Charlie Joiner and Kellen Winslow. The "Bolts" threw pass after pass after pass—all the way to two AFC championship games in the early 1980s.

Blue Notes

The popularity of the throwback jersey might be traced directly to the San Diego Chargers. Time after time the team's old, powder-blue AFL jerseys are voted among the best pro football uniforms of all time.

SAN FRANCISCO 49ERS

First Season: 1946

Franchise Record: 503–410–15
Home Field: Candlestick Park
(70,207 capacity) in San Francisco, California

CHAMPIONSHIPS
1981, 1984, 1988, 1989, 1994

In the 1980s two men changed the way championships were won in the NFL. Using a pass-first offense, coach Bill Walsh and quarterback Joe Montana led the San Francisco 49ers to victory. The team won five Super Bowls in 14 years.

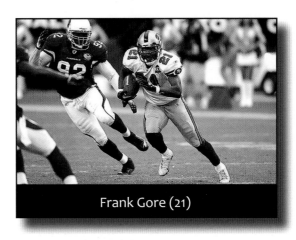
Frank Gore (21)

Legends & Stars

Jerry Rice

Roger Craig	RB	1983–1990	Scored three touchdowns in Super Bowl XIX
Ronnie Lott	DB	1981–1990	10-time Pro Bowl player
Joe Montana	QB	1979–1992	Led the 49ers to four Super Bowl wins
Joe Perry	FB	1948–1960	First NFL player to gain 1,000 yards in back-to-back seasons
Jerry Rice	WR	1985–2000	NFL's all-time leader in catches, yards, and touchdowns
Bill Walsh		1979–1988	49ers coach was an offensive genius and led San Francisco to three titles
Patrick Willis	LB	2007–present	Defensive Rookie of the Year named to Pro Bowl in first three seasons
Steve Young	QB	1987–1999	Followed Montana; was the most accurate quarterback in NFL history

By the Numbers

TOP PASSER	**Joe Montana** 1979–1992 35,124 yards	**TOP RUSHER**	**Joe Perry** 1948–1960 8,689 yards	
TOP RECEIVER	**Jerry Rice** 1985–2000 19,247 yards	**MOST TDS SCORED**	**Jerry Rice** 187 TDs	

"The Catch"

The most famous play in 49ers history didn't come in any of the team's Super Bowls. Instead, it was the play that got them to the big game for the first time. It happened with less than a minute left in the 1981 NFC championship game. Joe Montana threw a pass to the back corner of the end zone. Dwight Clark jumped up and reached as high as he could to grab the game-winning touchdown pass.

No Ordinary Joe

Joe Montana led 31 fourth-quarter comebacks in his career. None was more impressive than the 92-yard game-winning drive he managed in the closing moments of Super Bowl XXIII.

SEATTLE SEAHAWKS

First Season: 1976

Franchise Record: 255–277–0

Home Field: Qwest Field
(67,000 capacity) in Seattle, Washington

CHAMPIONSHIPS
None

When the NFL expanded in the late 1970s, it went to the one area of the United States that didn't have pro football—the Pacific Northwest. For more than three decades, the Seattle Seahawks have proved that the league made the right decision. Whether inside the Kingdome in the 1980s or outdoors at Qwest Field, the Seahawks have played in front of some of the loudest crowds in the game.

Legends & Stars

Matt Hasselbeck

Shaun Alexander	RB	2000–2007	Led the NFL in rushing and was named MVP in 2005
Kenny Easley	S	1981–1987	Named Defensive Player of the Year in 1984
Matt Hasselbeck	QB	2001–present	Took the Seahawks to Super Bowl XL in 2006
Cortez Kennedy	DT	1990–2000	Eight-time Pro Bowl pick and Defensive Player of the Year in 1992
Steve Largent	WR	1976–1989	Seven-time Pro Bowl selection

By the Numbers

TOP PASSER	**Matt Hasselbeck** 2001–present 26,433 yards	
TOP RECEIVER	**Steve Largent** 1976–1989 13,089 yards	
TOP RUSHER	**Shaun Alexander** 2000–2007 9,429 yards	
MOST TDS SCORED	**Shaun Alexander** 112 TDs	

Driving to the Big Game

There's a simple way to get to the Super Bowl: Give the ball to your best player. That's what the Seahawks did in the 2005 season. Running back Shaun Alexander carried the ball 34 times for 132 yards and two touchdowns against the Carolina Panthers during the championship game. At the end of the day, he carried the George Halas Trophy for the newly crowned NFC champions.

One for the Fans

The Seahawks have only two retired numbers: 80 for Steve Largent and 12 for their fans. The 12 represents the "12th man"—the loud, intimidating crowd that makes Qwest Field miserable for opposing players.

ST. LOUIS RAMS

First Season: 1937

Franchise Record: 504–483–20
Home Field: Edward Jones Dome
(66,000 capacity) in St. Louis, Missouri

CHAMPIONSHIPS
1945, 1951, 1999

Like a number of NFL teams, the Rams have moved around the country during their history. They were born in Cleveland and moved to Los Angeles in 1946. Then in 1995 they headed back to the Midwest, going to St. Louis. The Rams have won three championships in their history, one for each city.

Rams' touchdown celebration during Super Bowl XXXIV

Legends & Stars

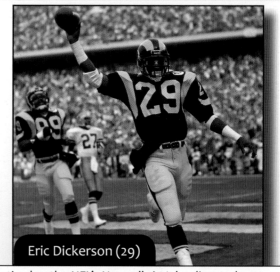

Eric Dickerson (29)

Eric Dickerson	RB	1983–1987	Retired as the NFL's No. 2 all-time leading rusher
Marshall Faulk	RB	1999–2005	Seven-time Pro Bowler and MVP in 2000
Elroy "Crazylegs" Hirsch	HB/E	1949–1957	Led the NFL in receiving and scoring in 1951
Steven Jackson	RB	2004–present	Two-time Pro Bowl pick
Deacon Jones	DE	1961–1971	Invented the term quarterback "sack" and racked up a lot of them long before it became an official stat
Kurt Warner	QB	1998–2003	MVP of Super Bowl XXXIV; NFL MVP in 1999 and 2001
Jack Youngblood	DE	1971–1984	Seven-time Pro Bowl selection played in 201 straight games

By the Numbers

TOP PASSER	**Jim Everett** 1986–1993 23,758 yards	**TOP RUSHER**	**Eric Dickerson** 1983–1987 7,245 yards
TOP RECEIVER	**Isaac Bruce** 1994–2007 14,109 yards	**MOST TDS SCORED**	**Marshall Faulk** 1999–2005 85 TDs

Greatest Show on Turf

From 1999 through 2001, the Rams were nearly unstoppable on offense. Quarterback Kurt Warner (13) won two MVPs, and running back Marshall Faulk won another. St. Louis won one Super Bowl and came up short in another. With Warner flinging the football all over the artificial grass at their home field, the Rams' circus act became known as "The Greatest Show on Turf."

Kurt Warner (13)

Fearsome Foursome

One of the most famous and dominating defensive lines in NFL history played for the Los Angeles Rams in the 1960s. Hall of Famers Merlin Olsen and Deacon Jones, along with Rosey Grier and Lamar Lundy, earned the nickname "The Fearsome Foursome."

TAMPA BAY BUCCANEERS

First Season: 1976

Franchise Record: 208–323–1
Home Field: Raymond James Stadium
(66,321 capacity) in Tampa, Florida

CHAMPIONSHIP
2002

They were once a laughingstock of pro football. They wore ugly orange uniforms, and it took them 27 tries to win their first game. But the Tampa Bay Buccaneers eventually turned things around. They changed their colors to a slick pewter and red and became the NFL champions of the 2002 season.

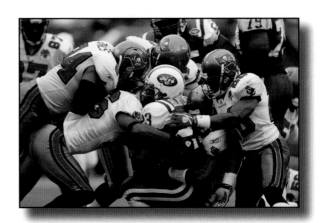

Legends & Stars

Warren Sapp (99)

Mike Alstott	FB	1996–2006	Bruising runner went to six Pro Bowls
Ronde Barber	DB	1997–present	Buccaneers' all-time leader in interceptions
Derrick Brooks	LB	1995–2008	11-time Pro Bowler was Defensive Player of the Year in 2002
Warren Sapp	DT	1995–2003	Sack master was named Defensive Player of the Year in 1999

By the Numbers

TOP PASSER	**Vinny Testaverde** 1987–1992 14,820 yards	**TOP RUSHER**	**James Wilder** 1981–1989 5,957 yards
TOP RECEIVER	**Mark Carrier** 1987–1992 5,018 yards	**MOST TDS SCORED**	**Mike Alstott** 1996–2006 71 TDs

Pickpocket Experts

The Buccaneers defeated the Oakland Raiders to win Super Bowl XXXVI. They picked off five passes and returned three of them for touchdowns. Dwight Smith took two back, and Derrick Brooks had the other. Defensive back Dexter Jackson, who had the Bucs' first two interceptions, was named the game's MVP.

Dexter Jackson (34)

Waiting to Win

In their first season, the Buccaneers failed to win a game, going 0–14. In their second season, they lost their first 12 games before finally tasting victory. The Bucs returned three interceptions for touchdowns in the road win over the New Orleans Saints. Fans were so excited about the victory that many greeted the players at the airport when they returned to Tampa.

TENNESSEE TITANS

Franchise Record: 371–379–6
Home Field: LP Field
(68,958 capacity) in Nashville, Tennessee

CHAMPIONSHIPS
1960 (AFL), 1961 (AFL)

First Season: 1960

Born as part of the American Football League, the Titans originally played in Texas and were known as the Houston Oilers. The Oilers moved north to Tennessee in 1997, but that's not oil country. So after two seasons, the team changed its name to the Titans, after the old AFL team, the New York Titans.

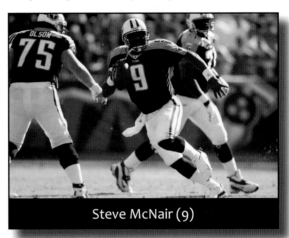
Steve McNair (9)

Warren Moon

Earl Campbell	RB	1978–1984	Three-time rushing champ was named NFL MVP in 1979
Ray Childress	DL	1985–1995	Five-time Pro Bowl selection
Chris Johnson	RB	2008–present	The 2009 NFL Offensive Player of the Year became the sixth running back to rush for 2,000 yards in a season
Bruce Matthews	OL	1983–2001	Played in an NFL-record 296 games over 19 seasons
Steve McNair	QB	1995–2005	Threw for 156 touchdowns and ran for 36 more
Warren Moon	QB	1984–1993	Ranked No. 3 on NFL's all-time passing list when he retired

By the Numbers

TOP PASSER	**Warren Moon** 1984–1993 33,685 yards	
TOP RECEIVER	**Ernest Givins** 1986–1994 7,935 yards	
TOP RUSHER	**Eddie George** 1996–2003 10,009 yards	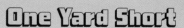
MOST TDS SCORED	**Eddie George** 74 TDs	

"Music City Miracle"

The greatest play in Titans' history might be one of the greatest plays in NFL history. It happened with the Titans trailing 16-15 with 16 seconds left in a 1999 playoff game in Nashville against the Buffalo Bills. Frank Wycheck caught a kickoff and tossed a lateral back and across the field to Kevin Dyson (87), who took it 75 yards for a touchdown and a Tennessee win.

One Yard Short

The Titans lost Super Bowl XXXIV in 2000 to the St. Louis Rams 23-16. They nearly forced overtime on the final play of the game when receiver Kevin Dyson caught a pass from Steve McNair. However, Dyson was tackled on the 1-yard line, just short of the end zone.

WASHINGTON REDSKINS

First Season: 1932

Franchise Record: 541–506–27

Home Field: FedEx Field
(91,665 capacity) in Landover, Maryland

CHAMPIONSHIPS
1937, 1942, 1982, 1987, 1991

The Redskins didn't always play in the nation's capital. Formed in 1932 as the Boston Braves, they changed their nickname a year later when they moved across town. In 1937 the team moved to Washington, D.C., and promptly won a championship that season. The franchise would go on to win four more championships over the next 60 years.

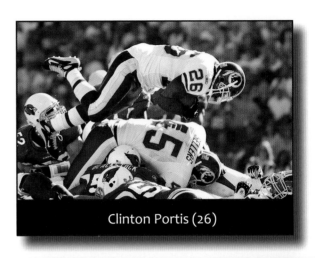
Clinton Portis (26)

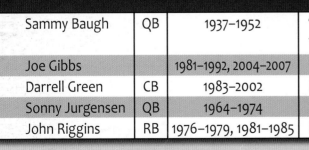
Legends & Stars

John Riggins

Sammy Baugh	QB	1937–1952	"Slingin' Sammy" was a six-time NFL passing leader in the 1930s and 1940s
Joe Gibbs		1981–1992, 2004–2007	Redskins coach led Washington to three Super Bowl titles
Darrell Green	CB	1983–2002	Intercepted 54 passes in his 20-year career
Sonny Jurgensen	QB	1964–1974	Five-time Pro Bowl pick led the NFL in passing three times
John Riggins	RB	1976–1979, 1981–1985	MVP of Super Bowl XVII

By the Numbers

TOP PASSER	**Joe Theismann** 1974–1985 25,206 yards	**TOP RUSHER**	**John Riggins** 1976–1979, 1981–1985 7,472 yards
TOP RECEIVER	**Art Monk** 1980–1993 12,026 yards	**MOST TDS SCORED**	**Charley Taylor** 1964–1975 90 TDs

Doug Williams Makes History

Each of Washington's three Super Bowl victories was won with a different starting quarterback. None was more significant than Doug Williams in Super Bowl XXII. Williams became the first African-American quarterback to start a Super Bowl game. He claimed MVP honors by throwing four touchdown passes in a 42-10 win over the Denver Broncos in 1988.

Devoted Fans

Since 1968 the Redskins have sold out every home game. That includes games played at D.C. Stadium (later called Robert F. Kennedy Memorial Stadium) and more recently, FedEx Field. It's the longest streak in the NFL.

Seattle Seahawks

Oakland Raiders

San Francisco 49ers

Denver Broncos

San Diego Chargers

Arizona
Cardinals

Dallas Cowboys

TEAM
MAP

Minnesota Vikings

Green Bay Packers

Detroit Lions

Buffalo Bills

New England Patriots

Chicago Bears

Cleveland Browns

Pittsburgh Steelers

New York Jets
New York Giants

Philadelphia Eagles

Baltimore Ravens

Washington Redskins

Indianapolis Colts

Cincinnati Bengals

Kansas City Chiefs

St. Louis Rams

Tennessee Titans

Carolina Panthers

Atlanta Falcons

Jacksonville Jaguars

New Orleans Saints

Houston Texans

Tampa Bay Buccaneers

Miami Dolphins

GLOSSARY

field goal—when the ball is kicked through the uprights for a score; a field goal is worth three points

interception—when a defensive player catches a quarterback's pass

pass—a forward throw of the ball from the quarterback to a receiver

reception—a catch

rush—another word for running with the ball after taking a handoff

sack—when the quarterback is tackled for negative yards while trying to pass

tackle—bringing a ball carrier to the ground, ending a play

touchdown—score when the ball is carried over the goal line and into the end zone; a touchdown is worth six points

FOOTBALL POSITIONS

C— center; the offensive lineman who snaps the ball to the quarterback

CB—cornerback; a defensive player who usually covers a wide receiver

DB—defensive back; any cornerback or safety

DE—defensive end; a lineman who often rushes the quarterback

DL—defensive lineman; any tackle, noseguard, or end

DT—defensive tackle; a lineman who covers the interior of the line

E—end; anyone who lines up on the end of the line; an older term for a receiver

F—flanker; a receiver who lines up behind the line of scrimmage

FB—fullback; a running back often used as a blocker

G—guard; an offensive lineman who lines up next to the center

HB—halfback; another name for a running back and is usually a ball carrier

K—kicker; a player who tries field goals and kicks off after scores and at the beginning of each half

LB—linebacker; a defensive player who lines up behind the linemen

OL—offensive lineman; a tackle, guard, or center who blocks for the ball carriers

P—punter; a player who kicks the ball to the opposing team after the offense has been stopped

QB—quarterback; the player who runs the offense, handing off and passing the ball

RB—running back; any player who carries the ball out of the backfield

S—safety; a defensive back who can cover an offensive player or help as the last line of defense

T—tackle; an offensive lineman who blocks defenders on the outside of the line

TE—tight end; an offensive lineman who is eligible to catch passes

WR—wide receiver; an offensive player who catches passes from the quarterback

READ MORE

Buckley, James, Jr., Jim Gigliotti, Matt Marini, and John Wiebusch. *The Child's World Encyclopedia of the NFL.* Mankato, Minn.: Child's World, 2007.

Buckman, Virginia. *Football Stars.* New York: Children's Press, 2007.

Christopher, Matt. *The Super Bowl.* New York: Little, Brown, 2006.

Pellowski, Michael. *The Little Giant Book: Football Facts.* New York: Sterling Pub., 2007.

INTERNET SITES

FactHound offers a safe, fun way to find Internet sites related to this book. All of the sites on FactHound have been researched by our staff.

Here's all you do:

Visit *www.facthound.com*

Type in this code: 9781429648196

INDEX